T0327144

WHY BELIEVE
IN JESUS'
RESURRECTION?

A little book of guidance

JAMES D. G. DUNN

First published in Great Britain in 2016

Society for Promoting Christian Knowledge
36 Causton Street
London SW1P 4ST
www.spck.org.uk

British Library Cataloguing-in-Publication Data
A catalogue record for this book is available from the British Library

ISBN 978–0–281–07658–1
eBook ISBN 978–0–281–07659–8

Typeset by Graphicraft Limited, Hong Kong
First printed in Great Britain by Ashford Colour Press
Subsequently digitally printed in Great Britain

Produced on paper from sustainable forests

Contents

About the author

James Dunn is Emeritus Lightfoot Professor of Divinity at Durham University, where he taught from 1982 to 2003. Previously, from 1970 to 1982, he was at the University of Nottingham. He has an MA and BD from the University of Glasgow, his alma mater, and a PhD and DD from the University of Cambridge, and is a Fellow of the British Academy (FBA). He is the author of over twenty monographs, including *Baptism in the Holy Spirit, Jesus and the Spirit, Unity and Diversity in the New Testament, Christology in the Making, The Partings of the Ways, The Theology of Paul the Apostle, The New Perspective on Paul, A New Perspective on Jesus, New Testament Theology: An Introduction, Did the First Christians Worship Jesus?, Jesus, Paul and the Gospels, The Oral Gospel Tradition,* and commentaries on Romans, Galatians, Colossians and Philemon, and Acts. His most recent work is a trilogy tracing the first 150 years of Christianity, *Christianity in the Making*. His doctoral pupils teach in many different parts of the world. He is married to Meta and they have three children. He functioned as a Methodist Local Preacher for forty years. He and his wife have now retired to Chichester to be nearer their daughters and worship at the local parish church.

Introduction

It's a most extraordinary claim, isn't it? That a man who lived 2,000 years ago died, but then rose from the dead! Of course, there are stories about individuals who died, or who were thought to have died, but who recovered. There are quite a number of such stories in most religions. For example, in the Old Testament the prophet Elisha restores the life of a Shunammite's child (2 Kings 4.32–37). And Jesus is recalled as restoring life to several individuals – notably Jairus' daughter (Mark 5) and the brother of Martha and Mary (John 11). Such stories can be classed as 'resurrection from the dead', although it is not always clear whether the central characters had actually died. So 'restoration to life' might be a better description. And those concerned had not actually defeated death, just postponed it. They would die later.

We should perhaps note that there are also claims that some individuals did not die but were transported directly to heaven, most notably Enoch and Elijah[1] – Elijah being one of two historically revered figures who early Christian tradition reports as meeting with Jesus on the mount of transfiguration (Mark 9.2–8). But they hardly provide a precedent for the claims regarding Jesus. So far as we can tell, no one doubted that Jesus did die on the cross. The crucifix has been a symbol of Christianity from very early times.

The distinctive and essential claim made regarding Jesus is that he had defeated death. He had died, but he had been raised to a life or existence *beyond* death, an existence over which death had no hold. He would not die again. Of course, the belief, or hope, that there is a life beyond death was already popular. But what that life was or consisted of was as unclear then as it still is today. And there are plenty of stories, both past and present, where someone who has died is seen active again, whether in dream or in vision. But, as we shall see, the stories regarding Jesus raised from the dead go beyond the usual category of such stories. So, what are we to make of them?

The debate about the Christian belief in Jesus' resurrection is, inevitably, rather complex. So we need to enter the debate with some caution. Caution is necessary, since the belief is truly extra-ordinary. In most controversies, special claims can usually be paralleled. The parallels are enough to indicate the plausibility of the claim. But if the claim is itself extraordinary, unparalleled, then the attempt to cite plausible parallels can only diminish the credibility of the claim itself. At the same time, the extraordinariness and lack of parallel should not count against the claim itself. We cannot deny a claim simply because it is extraordinary, otherwise we could hardly make sense, for example, of the beginning of the cosmos, or even of Alexander the Great's invasion of India. So, we must proceed with caution.

To start with, we should not fail to note that there are *no* accounts of Jesus' resurrection itself! Or at least, there are no accounts of Jesus' resurrection worth considering as first-hand accounts of his first followers. The only account as such from the early centuries of Christianity is in the Gospel of Peter,[2] which is so far removed from the Gospel accounts as to appear fanciful, and if anything highlights the soberness of the Gospel accounts. We will examine them below. But first we start with the record which the only first-hand witness gives us.

1

The (only) first-hand testimony

When did the belief that Jesus had been raised from the dead first emerge? The answer to this question is surprising. Surprising, because extraordinary claims about people regarded as famous usually take some time, even generations, to arise. But in the case of Jesus the belief that he had been raised from the dead emerged very soon after his death – indeed, as we shall see, within days of that death, according to the earliest testimonies. But we begin with what is in fact the only first-hand account.

This, the most striking personal testimony, is given by Paul. Paul, or as he was formerly known, Saul, had not been a disciple of Jesus. Indeed, he first appears in the story of Christianity's beginnings as a persecutor of the early Christians. According to the account of Christianity's beginnings in the Book of Acts,[1] as a zealous Pharisee, Saul had been evidently outraged by the claims that Jesus had been raised from the dead. So enraged, indeed, that he had tried to wipe out the belief. He first appears in the story of the first Christian martyr, Stephen, with the terse statement that 'Saul approved of their killing of him' (Acts 8.1). But it gets worse. 'Breathing threats and murder against the disciples' of Jesus, he had gone to the high priest in Jerusalem and been authorized to go to the synagogues of Damascus to arrest the followers of Jesus he found there (9.1–2).

It was on the road to Damascus, however, that he had, according to Luke, the author of Acts, encountered Jesus.

> Now as he was going along and approaching Damascus, suddenly a light from heaven flashed around him. He fell to the ground and heard a voice saying to him, 'Saul, Saul, why do you persecute me?' He asked, 'Who are you, Lord?' The reply came, 'I am Jesus, whom you are persecuting.'
> (Acts 9.3–5)

The story is vivid and dramatic. And one might be forgiven for wondering whether Luke had dramatized it, or indeed over-dramatized it.

Fortunately we have Paul's own account of the event. In one of history's most striking self-testimonies, Paul gives us what we might call the inner heart of the episode told so dramatically by Luke.

> I was violently persecuting the church of God and was trying to destroy it. I advanced in Judaism beyond many among my people of the same age, for I was far more zealous for the traditions of my ancestors. But when God, who had set me apart before I was born and called me through his grace, was pleased to reveal his Son in/to me, so that I might proclaim him among the Gentiles . . .
> (Galatians 1.13–16)

Paul's intention in this passage was evidently to contrast his pre-conversion zeal with his commitment to take the good news of Jesus beyond Israel, to 'proclaim him among the Gentiles'. But the sharpness of the contrast between his earlier zeal and his commitment to preach Christ is as striking as Luke's account in Acts 9. The slight confusion as to whether Paul's Greek should be translated as 'reveal his Son in me' or 'reveal his Son to me' may itself be some confirmation of an overwhelming episode in Paul's life.

It is notable that in providing the history of Christianity's beginnings (in the Acts of the Apostles) Luke recounts the story of Paul's conversion no fewer than three times.[2] It is understandable, of course, in that Paul was such an important Christian evangelist. Indeed, it was Paul's taking the good news (gospel)[3] of Jesus Christ well beyond Jewish circles, to the wider Gentile world, which ensured that Christianity would become an international religion and not just a form of Judaism. But the emphasis on Paul's conversion in Acts is nonetheless striking.

Prominent is the mention of light: 'a light from heaven' (9.3); 'a great light from heaven' (22.6); 'I could not see because of the brightness of that light' (22.11); 'a light from heaven, brighter than the sun' (26.13). Paul himself presumably reflects on an experience of such intensity when he writes to the Corinthians: 'It is the God who said, "Let light shine out of darkness", who has shone in our hearts to give the knowledge of the glory of God in the face of Jesus Christ' (2 Corinthians 4.6).

More important, of course, was the fact that Paul believed that he had been encountered by Jesus, a Jesus risen from the dead, on the road to Damascus. In the Acts accounts the claim is made ever more intense. In Acts 9 it is Ananias who comes to minister to Saul, blinded by the brightness of the light, who says, 'Brother Saul, the Lord Jesus, who appeared to you on your way here, has sent me' (Acts 9.17). In the Acts 22 account, presented as Paul's self-testimony, it is again Ananias who attests, 'The God of our ancestors has chosen you to know his will, to see the Righteous One and to hear his voice' (22.14). And most fully, in the third account, Paul himself attests (the risen) Jesus as commissioning him: 'for this purpose I have appeared to you, to appoint you as a servant and witness of what you have seen' (26.16). To which Paul adds: 'I was not disobedient to the heavenly vision' (26.19).

This emphasis Paul himself also underscores in his own self-testimony. In writing to the Corinthian church he underlines his authority in advising and rebuking the Corinthian believers. 'Am I not free? Am I not an apostle? Have I not seen Jesus our Lord? Are you not my work in the Lord?' (1 Corinthians 9.1).

There can be no doubt, then, that Saul, the persecutor of the first Christians, dramatically turned round 180 degrees, and became one of early Christianity's most effective missionaries and teachers. No doubt either that Paul himself attributed this astounding *volte-face* to what happened on his way to Damascus. Equally no doubt that Paul himself believed that he had encountered Jesus in that event. And that it was this encounter with the risen Jesus which had transformed him from a zealous opponent of the early movement into its most effective advocate that the good news of Jesus was for Gentiles as well as Jews.

Was Paul mistaken? That is certainly possible. But Paul was probably the sharpest mind among the earliest believers – a well-trained Pharisee[4] for a start. His focus on Christ, the repeated use of phrases like 'in Christ' and 'with Christ', all make sense in the light of his own memory of his conversion as an encounter with Jesus, risen from the dead. And suggestions that he had had a fit, or something similar, on the Damascus road make little sense when we recall how effectively he responded thereafter to the many complex challenges which he encountered in the churches he established.[5]

But let us look at the other evidence before making up our minds.

2

The earlier claims to encounter Jesus risen from the dead

The history of Christianity's beginnings in Acts is usually dated to the 80s of the first century. That is, probably over fifty years from Jesus' death. But Paul's references to his own conversion in his letters to the churches in Galatia and in Corinth are earlier – Galatians probably at the beginning of the 50s, and 1 Corinthians in the first half of the 50s. So that takes us back to something over twenty years from Jesus' death.

But one of the most striking pieces of evidence from that period is also given in 1 Corinthians, when Paul reminds his readers of the gospel which he first delivered to them.

I handed on to you as of first importance what I in turn had received: that Christ died for our sins in accordance with the scriptures, and that he was buried, and that he was raised on the third day in accordance with the scriptures, and that he appeared to Cephas, then to the twelve. Then he appeared to more than five hundred brothers at one time, most of whom are still alive, though some

> have died. Then he appeared to James, then to all the
> apostles. Last of all, as to one untimely born, he appeared
> also to me.   (1 Corinthians 15.3–8)

This takes us back still further. In the first place, Paul is
reminding the Corinthians of the gospel which he had first
proclaimed to them and which they had believed (15.11).
On the usual reckoning of Paul's missionary journeys, that
takes us back to about 50 CE,[1] when Paul first began his
mission to Corinth (Acts 18). But, of course, Paul is citing
a sequence of events which takes us still further back. These
events are usually referred to as 'resurrection appearances',
in which Jesus was remembered as having appeared
to various disciples after his death – they themselves, of
course, would say, 'after his death and resurrection'.

The last mentioned is the appearance which converted Paul himself. The fact that Paul introduces it as
'last of all' presumably means that there were no subsequent claims to have seen or been encountered by the
risen Jesus. That is interesting in itself. For if Paul's
conversion took place within a few years of Jesus' death,
that immediately means that first-hand testimony goes
back so far. It is not unimportant, then, to note that
belief that Jesus had been raised from the dead goes back
in first-hand testimony to within a few years of the event
claimed. Indeed, if Jesus was crucified in the year 30,[2]
Paul's own conversion is probably to be dated to 32 CE,
which would fit most comfortably with the likely dating
of the rest of his missionary work.

Paul refers to the appearance by which he was converted
not simply as 'last of all' but also 'as to one untimely born'

(*ektrōma*). His meaning is not entirely clear, but the most likely implication of *ektrōma*, 'premature birth, abortion', is that Paul fully recognized that most would regard his conversion to join those whom he had been persecuting as unnatural. Paul seems to accept this, recognizing that his claim to be an apostle, when he had not been a disciple of Jesus, but on the contrary a persecutor of Jesus' disciples, must seem as literally extra-ordinary. That Paul was nevertheless accepted by the first disciples of Jesus[3] must mean that they accepted his account of his conversion – as had the disciples in Damascus whom he had been sent to persecute (Acts 9.17–18)!

If a resurrection appearance in 32 CE had been 'late', the implication is that the earlier appearances in Paul's 1 Corinthians 15 list had been much earlier. In the account in Acts the appearances last for forty days (Acts 1.3), leaving a nice gap before Pentecost, fifty days after Passover and Easter. Other traditions grew up in different sects who wanted to attribute their own distinctive teaching to Jesus, by maintaining that Jesus' appearances went on for a much longer time.[4] But that longer period was almost certainly offered to help explain how the sect's new and distinctive teaching had emerged. The awkwardness of Paul's 'last of all' is probably sufficient to explain both the lateness of the appearance which he claimed and the gap between it and the earlier appearances.

The list of appearances prior to the appearance to Paul ends with an appearance 'to all the apostles' (15.7). This is distinguished from the appearance to 'the twelve' (15.5). So here we should remember that the word 'apostle' was more widely used in the earliest days of Christianity. An 'apostle' was one commissioned for particular ministry or to bear a particular responsibility. And Paul uses the term to describe a much wider range than the twelve, including Andronicus and Junia (Romans 16.7), Apollos (1 Corinthians 4.9), Barnabas (Galatians 2.8–9) and Silvanus (1 Thessalonians 2.6–7). So the reference here is presumably to a wide range of missionaries and responsibility bearers in the earliest churches. The reference seems to envisage a single appearance, but conceivably could have summarized a number of such commissioning appearances.

The appearance to James (1 Corinthians 15.7) has a particular poignancy. There were several men called James in the accounts of early Christianity. But no one doubts that the James referred to here was the brother[5] of Jesus, who quickly became leader of the church in Jerusalem,[6] quite possibly because he was Jesus' brother. There is no other reference in the New Testament to this appearance.

The appearance to 'more than five hundred' is equally unique in the 1 Corinthians 15 list (15.6). That such an appearance is recorded as happening before Christianity enjoyed its first burst of success, at Pentecost following Luke's account of appearances (Acts 2), is somewhat strange. Perhaps it suggests, as we shall see, that the 1 Corinthians 15 sequence of appearances went beyond Luke's 'forty days'. And that Luke chose to complete the period of appearances before the first Christian Pentecost, to avoid any confusion. At any rate, the list provided by Paul, which he insists is entirely reliable (1 Corinthians 15.1–3), is probably a surer testimony than Luke's version at this point.

The first two appearances in Paul's list are those first to Peter and then to the twelve (15.5). The appearance to Peter by himself is otherwise mentioned in the New Testament only in Luke 24.34. But it helps explain why Peter emerged as such a leading figure in Acts, despite his denial of Jesus when the latter was on trial (Mark 14.66–72). And appearances to the twelve[7] are the most widely but variously recorded of all the appearance traditions.[8]

According to the Gospels and Acts there were other appearances – notably, of course, to the women who went to the tomb of Jesus to anoint his body (Mark 16.1). Somewhat oddly, Mark does not record any appearance, but records that the women 'saw a young man' in the tomb who pointed them forward to appearances in the near future (16.7). Matthew follows Mark, but adds the record of an appearance to the women as they ran away from the empty tomb (Matthew 28.9–10). Somewhat oddly, Luke does not record any appearances at the tomb, but largely follows Mark's account (Luke 24.4–9) and later in the same chapter refers to the women at the tomb having 'a vision of angels' (24.23). That reference back comes at the beginning of a lengthy account of a disciple called Cleopas and a companion on the road to Emmaus, who encounter and are joined by a man whom they latterly recognize to be Jesus (24.31). On returning to Jerusalem to tell their story they learn that 'The Lord has risen indeed, and has appeared to Simon (Peter)' (24.35). Luke's account goes on to record an appearance of Christ in Jerusalem the same evening (24.36–43). And both Matthew and Luke conclude their accounts with Jesus commissioning the disciples to preach in his name and make disciples of all nations (Matthew 28.18–20; Luke 24.47–49).

In Luke's second volume (Acts 1.1–8), the commissioning is elaborated in terms of an empowering by the Holy Spirit shortly to be given to them (at Pentecost – Acts 2). That is followed by an account of Jesus' ascension to heaven, evidently intended as marking the end of the forty days during which the risen Jesus moved about among his disciples before on each occasion disappearing.

John's account is quite different. Mary Magdalene (the reformed prostitute?) is encountered by (a risen) Jesus, whom she does not at first recognize. When she does recognize him, Jesus tells her not to 'hold on' to him, because he has not yet 'ascended to the Father' (John 20.11–18). So Matthew and John agree that the first to see the risen Jesus was Mary Magdalene, along with another Mary according to Matthew. John then records an appearance to 'the disciples' on the same (Sunday) evening, in which Jesus commissions them – 'As the Father has sent me, so I send you' (20.21), authorizing them to forgive or retain the sins of others (20.23). Uniquely John records a second appearance to the disciples, a week later (20.26–29). The occasion is prompted by the fact that Thomas had not been present the first time, and was unpersuaded by his fellow-disciples' testimony. On this second occasion Jesus invites Thomas to put his finger in the imprints of the crucifixion nails in his hands and his hand in Jesus' side, where his already dead body had suffered a spear-thrust when on the cross (19.33–34). Thomas apparently does not accept the challenge but acknowledges Jesus as 'My Lord and my God' (20.28).

In what appears to be a chapter added to the earlier draft of his Gospel (John 21), there follow accounts of

Jesus appearing to his disciples in Galilee, when they had gone fishing. The principal objective is evidently to recount the restoration of Peter to a leading position among the disciples. He is asked three times whether he loves Jesus, recalling his triple denial of Jesus on the outskirts of Jesus' trial (18.15–18, 25–27). And when he reaffirms his love for Jesus, he is told to feed Jesus' sheep (21.15–17). The implication is that Peter was thus restored to his position as Jesus' leading disciple and given the principal pastoral responsibility within the church and the mission which was soon to emerge.

3

What are we to make of the tensions between the several accounts?

Thus far we have simply provided brief descriptions of the various accounts of what are generally referred to as Jesus' 'resurrection appearances'. There are several issues to be considered.

(a) Were the first appearances to women, as Matthew and John indicate? And if so, why does Paul not mention them in the list of appearances he cites at the beginning of 1 Corinthians 15?

The answer to the second question may be straight-forward. The testimony of women was not so highly valued in first-century society as that of men.[1] But the list on which Paul drew, and to which he added his own experience in 1 Corinthians 15, was probably intended to function as reliable and trustworthy testimony, of legal weight. In which case, to give the testimony of women first place in the list of reliable witnesses would presumably be regarded as diminishing the value and weight of the testimony. Since Paul himself greatly valued the contribution and support of women in his own mission,[2] the fact that he ignores the role of women as witnesses to Jesus' resurrection is probably due to his drawing on a tradition already edited to enhance its social and legal force. That there may have been some concern to give the appearance to Cephas/Peter primacy in the record of appearances is a further factor which should not be ignored.

Another explanation for the omission of the women's testimony may be the inconsistencies and confusion in or between the various accounts. It is hard, for a start, to reconcile the accounts of the Synoptic Gospels, that there was no appearance at the tomb, with John's rather moving account of the appearance to Mary Magdalene at the tomb. Matthew's account of an initial appearance to the two Marys as they ran away from the tomb only adds to the confusion on this point. And it is notable, as also surprising, that no women are mentioned in subsequent appearances. Or was Cleopas' companion in Luke 24 a woman? The contrast between John's somewhat fulsome account of the appearance to Mary in John 20.11–18 and his silence about women sharing in the subsequent appearances is rather striking. It is hard to avoid the suspicion that the same concern which restricted the number of testimonies of 1 Corinthians 15 was also a factor in restricting the accounts of subsequent appearances. That the accounts of Matthew and John exist, of appearances to women at or near the tomb – the first appearances before any others – is probably an indication of the earliest churches' readiness to acknowledge and celebrate their testimony within their own communities rather than to put them forward as reliable witnesses to persuade others.

(b) Are the appearances properly described as 'visions' – the word used in Paul's description of his Damascus road conversion (Acts 26.19)? Or were they as 'physical' as Luke's and John's accounts would seem to imply?

In Luke's account the risen Jesus seems to be unremarkable to Cleopas and his companion. He walks with them to Emmaus speaking at length with them. He sits at table with them and breaks bread, before vanishing out of their sight (Luke 24.25–31). In the following appearance in Jerusalem Jesus calms the apprehensions of the disciples that they were seeing a spirit. He invites them to 'see my hands and my feet, that it is I myself; handle me, and see; for a spirit has not flesh and bones as you see that I have' (24.39). And since they still disbelieved and wondered, Jesus takes a piece of broiled fish offered to him and eats it before them (24.41–43). Furthermore, in the introduction to the Acts sequel, Luke implies that Jesus instructed the disciples during the whole forty-day period before his ascension. 'He presented himself alive to them by many convincing proofs, appearing to them during forty days and speaking about the kingdom of God' (Acts 1.3).

In John's account the risen Jesus says intriguingly to Mary at the tomb, 'Do not hold on to me, because I have not yet ascended to the Father' (John 20.17). In the second appearance to the disciples, as already noted, Jesus invites Thomas to 'Put your finger here and see my hands. Reach out your hand and put it in my side' (20.27), although Thomas apparently did neither but simply worshipped him (20.28). And in the sequel Jesus has apparently lit a charcoal fire and cooks fish for the disciples – the bread and fish perhaps an echo of the last supper which Jesus had celebrated with his disciples before his betrayal and crucifixion (21.9–13).[3]

The sheer physicality of these accounts is notable. All the more notable, indeed, since the feature seems to be at some remove from Paul's very clear conviction that the resurrection body is *not* physical. Indeed he takes some pains to make the point in 1 Corinthians 15. In a sustained sequence of contrasts (15.42–54) he makes repeated sharp distinctions between the 'natural body' (of this life) and the 'spiritual body' of the resurrection – for example, 'corruption'/'incorruption' (15.42, 50), 'weakness'/ 'power' (15.43), 'earthly'/'heavenly' (15.47–49), 'mortal'/ 'immortal' (15.54). In this sequence Paul clearly understands 'flesh and blood' (15.50) to characterize the natural body, in contrast to the resurrection body. This is evidently at some odds with the accounts of Luke and John, which seem intent to emphasize the physical reality of Jesus' resurrection. Is it simply that Paul could not but be mindful of the typical Greek assumption that spirit and flesh were poles apart? In which case he could well have recognized that a too physical understanding of Jesus' resurrection would be unpersuasive to a Greek audience. Indeed, it is one of the great failures of subsequent Christianity that Paul's distinction between 'flesh' and 'body' was lost to sight, and that Paul's negative attitude to 'flesh' (as in the antithesis between 'flesh' and 'spirit') was extended to include bodily and sexual function. On the other hand, we might wonder whether Paul was too concerned to address Greek prejudices and whether his account should be regarded effectively as a critique of Luke's and John's accounts of Jesus' resurrection appearances.

(c) Where did the appearances take place – Jerusalem or Galilee?

Mark's account anticipates appearances in Galilee, to which the disciples are directed (Mark 16.7), with no implication that there will be appearances elsewhere. The initial appearances in Matthew are to the women departing from the tomb, but the message they are given is that the disciples should go to Galilee 'and there they will see me' (Matthew 28.10). The 'great commission' which then follows, and which concludes Matthew's account, takes place in Galilee (28.16). Luke, on the other hand, links Mark's reference to an appearance in Galilee to a promise given earlier in Galilee (Luke 24.6). And the appearances which he goes on to relate all take place near to or in Jerusalem itself (24.13–53). Indeed, Luke seems to allow no room for appearances in Galilee! Perhaps he just decided to ignore such reports in order to keep the focus on Jerusalem, simply because he saw the early mission as moving out in increasing circles from an initial centre in Jerusalem (Acts 1.8).

John complicates the issue by having the disciples lingering in Jerusalem at least for a week following the initial appearances (John 20). But John 21 switches the narrative abruptly to Galilee. The disciples seem to be unsure what to do (21.2–3), so what the commissioning of 20.22–23 would have meant for them is hardly clear. And presumably the disciples' readiness to return to their own trade of fishing raises similar questions. Indeed, John's account of Jesus' commissioning of the disciples on Easter Sunday ('Receive the Spirit' – 20.22) does not entirely leave need or room for a further anointing with the Spirit (Pentecost)! And John seems to have no qualms in ending his Gospel in Galilee, making no attempt to swing the focus back to Jerusalem.

In some contrast, apart from a couple of references back to the earlier phase of Jesus' mission (Acts 10.37; 13.31), Luke refers to Galilee on only one further occasion, as a region where 'the church' was established and grew (9.31). This slight possible confusion on the 'where' of the appearances has naturally raised questions as to whether Jerusalem was the only centre of Christianity's beginnings (as Acts clearly implies). Or should Galilee, where Jesus had been most successful in his mission, be regarded as a separate initiating centre of the Jesus movement, even if it was soon absorbed by the mission emerging from Jerusalem? The answer is hardly very clear, but the question itself may not be very important in the event.

(d) How long was the period in which resurrection appearances were remembered as taking place?

Luke, of course, is quite clear – 'forty days' (Acts 1.3). But the tradition which Paul cites does not provide any timing for the appearances, apart from the 'last of all' of the appearance to Paul himself (1 Corinthians 15.5–8). The appearances to Cephas/Peter and to the twelve (15.5) can be readily set within the forty-day period of Luke's record, and presumably also the appearance to James (15.7). But when did the appearance to 'more than five hundred brothers' (15.6) take place? The question naturally arises because 'more than five hundred' surely implies that the Jesus movement had already begun to expand. There is no other indication that prior to Pentecost the disciples were more than a relatively small group (Acts 1.13–15). If, however, the Acts 2 account is to be taken in straightforward terms, the number who responded to Peter's Pentecost sermon and were converted was 'about three thousand persons' (2.41). So an appearance to more than five hundred could well be envisaged some time thereafter. But in timing, Pentecost is already beyond Luke's 'forty days'. Of course, Luke may simply have wanted to present a tidier picture of Christianity's beginnings – with a clear gap between Jesus' ascension (ending the sequence of appearances?) and Pentecost. So, perhaps the issue should not be pushed too hard, and perhaps Luke himself would not have wanted to insist that the appearance to the more than five hundred took place within his forty days.

Of the further appearances mentioned in 1 Corinthians 15 the one to 'all the apostles' is the other striking testimony hard to fit with Luke's forty days. For, as we have already seen, the appearance to 'all the apostles' is not to be identified with the appearance to 'the twelve', and 'the apostles' were a wider group than 'the twelve'. Of the former, Andronicus and Junia may well have been appointed by the risen Christ within the forty days, since Paul says that they 'were in Christ' before him (Romans

16.7). And Barnabas was an early disciple (Acts 4.36–37) who also sponsored Paul and quieted the suspicions of the others when the converted Paul first came to Jerusalem (9.26–27). So if Barnabas was an 'apostle' by virtue of being appointed by the risen Christ in a personal commissioning appearance, then the appearance to him could also have taken place during Luke's forty days.

But Apollos does not appear on the scene until Acts 18.24. And 'he knew only the baptism of John' and had to be more fully instructed by Priscilla and Aquila (18.25–26). So it is very unlikely that he can be numbered among those favoured with appearances during Acts' forty days in Jerusalem. Similarly Silvanus does not appear until later in Paul's story,[4] though if Silvanus was also known as Silas, he first appears as a messenger of the Jerusalem leadership in Acts 15.22. Of course, the word 'apostle' was also used to denote a person commissioned to represent a church in some business or negotiation.[5] But all those already personally mentioned were 'apostles' in the fuller sense – those commissioned by the risen Lord and church-founders. In particular, Paul's references to Apollos in 1 Corinthians[6] certainly seem to imply that his role as a church-founder was more or less equivalent to Paul's.

Most probably, then, we have to infer that the attested resurrection appearances were spread over a longer period than Luke's convenient forty days (prior to Pentecost). And since the implied apostle-appointing appearance to Apollos in particular seems to have been so unusual ('he knew only the baptism of John'), we probably have to infer that it took place outside the circle of appearances in Jerusalem and Galilee recorded by the Evangelists and Paul. As awkward as these inferences are, they at least help to explain why Paul's claim to a converting/commissioning appearance, which fell well outside the forty days and the traditions of appearances in Jerusalem and Galilee, could have been accepted as readily as it was. It can also be regarded as a positive sign, regarding the weight of the testimony, that no one seems to have been concerned to remove such unclarity and confusion. There is a rawness in the testimony which goes some way to attest its genuineness.

In sum, then, what is striking is the fact that those responsible for forming and passing on the earliest Christian traditions did not seem to be concerned about what appear to the observer to be curiosities and inconsistencies in this most important testimony that the first believers could give. Was this simply because these traditions came from different individuals and groups and had become well established before they were written down? Certainly Luke insists that he got his information from eyewitnesses and that he had investigated everything carefully from the very first (Luke 1.3). But the very fact that it is Luke who effectively ignores the traditions of appearances in Galilee makes one wonder whether he had any concerns regarding the detail and facticity of some of the reports he had gleaned.

The question whether the appearances were actual visions, or only visionary, is also raised by the language used ('vision') in the accounts themselves. The appearance to Paul can certainly be so described, as Acts 26.19

indicates.[7] And the abruptness with which Jesus appears and disappears, explicit in some accounts,[8] raises a similar question. But the accounts of the physicality or substantiality of Jesus' resurrected presence given by Luke and John would have to be wholly discounted before an 'only or merely visionary' assessment could be properly registered. And the one who gives first-hand testimony of seeing the risen Jesus (1 Corinthians 9.1) was evidently no stranger to 'visions and revelations' (2 Corinthians 12.1–7). So the first believers in Jesus' resurrection were no doubt aware that their testimony could be challenged as merely visionary. And yet they evidently promulgated the list of appearances which Paul cites in 1 Corinthians 15 with all the confidence of those who knew that their lives had been transformed by these experiences.

But let us press back still further, to the testimony that Jesus' tomb was found empty on the first Easter Sunday.

4

The empty tomb tradition

The earliest Christian testimony is straightforward and clear. During the Passover celebrations in Jerusalem Jesus had been arrested, tried and condemned to be crucified (Mark 14—15). All four Gospels agree that Joseph of Arimathea, a respected councillor, took the responsibility of asking the Roman Governor, Pilate, for his permission to bury the body of the crucified Jesus.[1] Permission granted, Joseph took Jesus' body down from the cross, wrapped it in a linen shroud, and laid it in a tomb hewn in the rock which he had prepared for his own burial. The entrance to the tomb was then covered by a great stone.[2] This is the basic story on which all four Evangelists agree, with varied details which simply indicate how varied was the retelling of the story and raise no questions as to the reliability of the primary detail. Most striking is the fact that Joseph of Arimathea, an evidently respected figure, is not mentioned anywhere else in the New Testament. This probably increases the credibility of the account. It was not the burial which was controversial, but what happened thereafter.

The accounts of Matthew, Mark and Luke include the note that women followers of Jesus observed where Jesus' body was laid.[3] This is in preparation for the following account that, after the Sabbath day of rest, they returned to the tomb to anoint the body (Mark 16.1; Luke 24.1). John's account confuses the issue somewhat since it notes that Nicodemus had brought spices with him and that they had already anointed Jesus' dead body with spices 'according to the burial custom of the Jews' (John 19.40). Such a confusion or misunderstanding hardly puts a question mark against the accounts, though if John had been able to draw on a personal account of such a leading figure in the Jerusalem community, it is somewhat surprising that Nicodemus is not mentioned elsewhere – though neither is Joseph. The accounts certainly raise questions, but since the subsequent histories of Joseph and Nicodemus are unknown it is difficult to inquire effectively as to why they disappear from the picture, or at least are not mentioned again following this basic service or act of humanity.

The key testimony is that on the Sunday morning when the women came to the tomb they found that the 'great stone' (Matthew 27.60) or 'very large' stone (Mark 16.4) had been rolled away from the door of the tomb.[4] Matthew alone adds the not insignificant detail that 'there was a great earthquake; for an angel of the Lord descended from heaven and came and rolled back the stone' (Matthew 28.2). Is this an example of Matthew's (over-)dramatization of an account which was otherwise straightforward, despite the astonishing claim being made?

The simplest account, not altogether surprisingly, is the earliest – Mark's. He has the women, Mary Magdalene, Mary the mother of James, and Salome, coming early on the Sunday to anoint Jesus' body with spices (Mark 16.1–2). While Mary Magdalene is a regular feature in all the accounts,[5] Mary the mother of James is a somewhat obscure figure.[6] Was she 'the mother of James and Joses' (Matthew 27.56; Mark 15.40)? Was she 'the other Mary' of Matthew 27.61 and 28.1? Why is she referred to simply as 'the mother of Joses' in Mark 15.47, and as 'the mother of James' in 16.1? And what about Salome, who is mentioned only in Mark 15.40 and 16.1? And then there is Joanna, mentioned only in Luke 24.10. Is the confusion simply the result of these testimonies being regarded as of insufficient weight in themselves (so not included in any way in the 1 Corinthians 15 list), and therefore rather neglected?

Certainly these differences can be, at least in part, attributed to confused and varied memories. That such an event as the discovery of the tomb no longer occupied should have caused confusion is hardly surprising. And the greater attention very quickly being given to accounts of Jesus' appearances, and then to their ordering in sequence (of importance?), naturally suggests that much less attention was given to the accounts of the tomb being found empty and by whom. Here it is probably significant that the 1 Corinthians 15 formal statement of earliest Christian belief in Jesus' resurrection makes no mention of the empty tomb. So the confusion in the remembering of what the women found and who they were is probably simply that: confusion in details which were considered relatively less important in themselves. That the consequence was a confusion and even some disagreement in the details remembered and recorded is regrettable indeed, but otherwise entirely understandable. The key fact, that the tomb was empty, remains undisputed.

Another problematic feature is the presence of angels in the account. In Matthew the rolling away of the stone to uncover the mouth of the tomb is attributed to an angel descended from heaven. 'His appearance was like lightning and his raiment white as snow' (Matthew 28.2–3). The angel sets the women's fears at rest, invites them to look into the tomb to see where Jesus had lain, and commissions them to go and tell Jesus' disciples that he has risen and will go before them to Galilee (28.5–7). Somewhat similar, Luke has the women first looking into the tomb and finding no body (Luke 24.2–3). While perplexed, 'two men stood by them in dazzling apparel'. They ask in resonant words: 'Why do you seek the living among the dead?', and remind the women of what Jesus had said 'while he was still in Galilee', that his death was foreordained (Luke 24.5–7).

Mark, however, has no angels – probably, we should add, no angels as such. When the women enter the tomb 'they saw a young man sitting on the right side, dressed in a white robe'. He reassures them that Jesus has risen, and gives more or less the same instructions as the angel in Matthew (Mark 16.5–7). The reference to 'a young man' (*neaniskos*) recalls Mark's only other use of the word, in 14.51, where he alone of the Evangelists notes that 'a certain young man' was close by when Jesus was arrested, and that he escaped when the soldiers tried to seize him, running off naked. Inevitably, one can hardly help wondering whether Mark was signalling that he himself had anticipated the women coming to the tomb and was in fact the 'young man' who announced to them the news of Jesus' resurrection.

John certainly includes no angels, but he has a more intriguing account of the discovery of the empty tomb (John 20.1–10). Mary Magdalene is the sole discoverer that the stone has been removed from the tomb. She runs at once to tell the news to Simon Peter and the disciple 'whom Jesus loved'. They in turn run to the tomb. The other disciple reaches it first, but does not enter. Peter it is who catches up and enters, to see only the grave clothes in place – the body itself having disappeared. They then return to their homes. This is an interesting way of giving primacy to the testimony of Peter; though, of course, John does not attribute the initial appearance of the risen Jesus to Peter, but rather to Mary (20.11–18).

So, what are we to make of all this? The first Christians, of course, were convinced that Jesus had been raised from the dead. This quickly became one of their basic confessions: that God had raised Jesus from the dead on the third day.[7] This indeed was the central claim of the earliest Christian preaching, and it was acceptance of this claim and belief in/commitment to this risen Lord Jesus which was the principal bond binding Jew and Gentile alike in the formation of the earliest churches. And, of course, although the empty tomb tradition may have been neglected, relative to the accounts of the risen Jesus appearing, it remained a fundamental element in the whole record and remembrance of how the belief in Jesus as risen Lord had itself first arisen.

Understandably, then, the empty tomb tradition is central and fundamental to this basic Christian belief. And, equally understandably, various alternative explanations have been given. The claim itself is so exceptional that it would be very surprising if other explanations had not been suggested.

One of the earliest alternative explanations has been given us by Matthew. He complicates the story of Jesus' burial and the discovery of the empty tomb (Matthew 27.62–66) by noting that the chief priests and Pharisees had asked for a guard to be posted at the tomb. According to Matthew this was to ensure that Jesus' disciples did not remove the body in order to be able to claim that he had risen from the dead. The request was granted and a guard of soldiers was posted to secure the site. Since Matthew is the only one to include this detail, he also has to include the note that when the stone was rolled away from covering the entrance to the tomb by 'an angel of the Lord' the guards were terrified 'and became like dead men' (28.2–4). Matthew makes no attempt to mention any interaction between the women and the guards, but completes his account by having some of the guard reporting back to the chief priests. The guards are then bribed to report that while they slept Jesus' disciples had come by night and stolen away Jesus' body. Matthew concludes this report, unique to his Gospel, by noting that this was the story which had been 'spread among the Jews to this day' (28.11–15).

The problem with this explanation for the spread of the belief that Jesus had been raised from the dead is obvious. If Jesus' disciples had removed Jesus' dead body from Joseph's tomb, they would have had to rebury it in another tomb. They certainly would not have disposed of it by simply throwing it into some burial site for vagrants and criminals. But if another tomb or burial site is to be considered, what one and where? Given that the Jesus movement began to 'take off' soon after, it is entirely unlikely that Jesus' disciples would just ignore the site where his body lay. On the contrary, and inevitably, the place or tomb of burial of such a revered teacher would have become a sacred site. How could the first Christians have failed to want to honour the site where Jesus' body lay? But no other site has been identified. It hardly makes sense to replace the incredibility of resurrection with the incredibility of another burial site which no one cared enough to remember, mark or honour.

Here it is necessary only to note that the Church of the Holy Sepulchre in Jerusalem, the traditional site of Jesus' burial, was built on the orders of the first Christian Emperor, Constantine, issued in 325/326. Since the area where the church was built lay outside the first-century walls of Jerusalem, and had been used for tombs, a hill having been levelled for the construction, the site has about as much plausibility as could be hoped for. Other sites for the original tomb of Jesus have been suggested, but hardly with the same credibility. The Garden Tomb, favourite of many Christian visitors to Jerusalem, was only suggested in the nineteenth century, on the grounds that it resembled a skull, and so could be identified with

Golgotha 'which means the place of a skull'.[8] Even less credibility can be attributed to the Talpiot tomb, five kilometres south of the old city of Jerusalem, only discovered in 1980.

The puzzle, then – if not that tomb, then where and what burial or disposal place? – points more to the authenticity of the Gospels' own empty tomb story than to any other explanation. There is an alternative suggestion – that it was the wrong tomb to which the women came. But that can hardly be fitted into the data which has come down to us. There is a distinctiveness about the account of Joseph of Arimathea's role which is hard to escape, and similarly the concern of the women to ensure that Jesus' body was properly anointed. And the question as to where Jesus' body really was finally laid still poses an inescapable problem. For if Jesus' tomb was actually undisturbed, then it is hardly possible to credit that no one pointed this out, that no agents of the high priests sought out Jesus' actual burial site and exposed the falsehood of Jesus' disciples' claim. So that alternative explanation seems to be even less credible than the former.

And much the same verdict has to be given to a third explanation – that Jesus had not really died and had recovered sufficiently to escape from the tomb and to convince his disciples that he was alive (again). But it is hardly more persuasive as an explanation of the earliest Christian belief in Jesus' resurrection. That Jesus did in fact die on the cross makes best sense, given the horrific scourging and beatings to which he had been subjected.[9] The spear-thrust of the Roman soldier into the side of the crucified Jesus, according to John 19.34–35, would have hastened that death. Even if he had recovered while lying in the tomb, it is scarcely credible that he could have freed himself from any burial wrappings or been able from the inside to roll back the stone covering the mouth of the tomb. And would a half-dead Jesus have been able to persuade his followers that he had actually risen from the dead? Nor should we forget that the same problem just discussed re-emerges here too. For if Jesus had simply recovered from his scourging and crucifixion, then he would have had to die some time thereafter. And we are back to the problem that no (other) tomb or resting place for Jesus' body can be identified with any credibility.

So, on balance, it seems hard to contradict the Gospels' accounts that the tomb where Jesus' dead body was laid was subsequently (two days later) found to be empty. Of course, the whole story could be dismissed as made up and untrue. But if its testimony is taken seriously, then despite individual oddities, it is hard to escape the conclusion: that on the Sunday following Jesus' crucifixion, the tomb in which his dead body had been laid was found to be empty.

5

Why 'resurrection'?

For a tomb to be found empty, and only two days after a body had been placed in it, the most obvious answer to the puzzle would seem to be one of the three that have just been discussed. It was empty because the body had been removed/stolen. It was empty because it was the wrong tomb. It was empty because Jesus had recovered sufficiently to escape from the tomb. But if these explanations of the empty tomb lack credibility, how much more credible is the claim that Jesus had been raised from the dead?

For a start, where did the very idea of resurrection come from? We know that the hope of resurrection only became prominent among Israelites in the period known as late Second Temple Judaism. It is most clearly indicated in what is usually reckoned as a late (fourth century BCE) addition to the prophecy of Isaiah (Isaiah 24—27) and in Daniel 12.1–3.

> Your dead shall live, their corpses shall arise. O dwellers in the dust, awake and sing for joy! For your dew is a radiant dew, and the earth will give birth to those long dead. (Isaiah 26.19)

35

> At that time Michael, the great prince, the protector of
> your people, shall arise. There shall be a time of anguish,
> such as has never occurred since nations first came into
> existence. But at that time your people shall be delivered,
> everyone who is found written in the book. Many of
> those who sleep in the dust of the earth shall awake, some
> to everlasting life, and some to shame and everlasting
> contempt. Those who are wise shall shine like the bright-
> ness of the sky, and those who lead many to righteousness,
> like the stars for ever and ever.   (Daniel 12.1–3)

The earliest expressions of martyr-theology already include
hope of vindication in terms of resurrection (2 Maccabees
7.9, 14). The Sadducees, the priestly party in first-century
Israel, did not believe in resurrection, as the episode in
Jesus' life indicates (Mark 12.18–27). But the Pharisees,
the other prominent party in Second Temple Judaism,
were already convinced, as Acts 23.6–8 makes clear.[1]
And the Mark 12 passage indicates that Jesus shared the
Pharisees' belief.

So, if Jesus had hoped for vindication, despite and
following the rejection he seems to have anticipated, it
is entirely likely that he would have expressed this hope
in terms of resurrection. This is certainly how the first
Christians remembered Jesus as expressing that hope –
most notably in the three 'Passion predictions' in Mark.[2]
But presumably the resurrection hoped for was resurrection
as it was understood in late Second Temple Judaism –
that is, resurrection at the end of the present age, resurrection as part of what becomes known in Christian thinking
as the general resurrection. And if Jesus expected or hoped
for that resurrection 'after three days', does that mean

that he thought he was about to enter the final phase of
world history, of the world as it was then known?

This raises one of the trickiest and possibly most
embarrassing aspects of earliest Christian belief. I refer
to the conviction which seems to have been common
among the first Christians, that Jesus would return again
in glory. And not just that, but also that he would return
within a short time. The belief that the risen Jesus
was the 'first fruits', that is, the beginning of the harvest
of the general resurrection, was evidently widely shared
(1 Corinthians 15.20–23). That those who had com-
mitted themselves to Christ would soon share in his
resurrection was clearly widely believed (Romans 8.22–
23). They were just waiting for it to happen, as happen
it soon would (1 Thessalonians 1.10; 4.13–18). This was
evidently a dominant hope (1 Corinthians 7.29–31), and
early Christian worship would often have been punctu-
ated by the cry, 'Maranatha – our Lord come!' (16.22).

The point, then, is that the first disciples of Jesus seem
to have used the language of resurrection to describe what
they believed had happened that first Easter. In the first
place, they were prompted by the discovery that Jesus'
tomb was empty to conclude that he had been raised
from the dead. Whether this interpretation of the empty
tomb was the result of Jesus having expressed the hope of
vindication following his rejection and death is hardly
very clear. Apart from anything else, the empty tomb
and following appearances are remembered as wholly
unanticipated and surprising. Was it then some revelation/
conviction which emerged from the discovery that the
tomb was empty? So the empty tomb stories tell us –

initially through angelic attestation. But whatever the reason, the belief that Jesus had been raised from the dead quickly became established among the first disciples, and became, indeed, the principal and convincing claim in their preaching thereafter.

Was the interpretation wrong? The fact that what they believed had happened to Jesus was *not* the beginning of the end of the age, was not the 'first fruits' of general resurrection, as the image of 'first fruits' would usually signify, was doubtless embarrassing. Even more embarrassing, now that nearly 2,000 years have elapsed since then! But did the failure of that imagery, that metaphor, to be realized, as its initial use assumed would be the case, mean that the metaphor should be dropped? Such a conclusion was never seriously considered so far as we can tell. Why, for example, did the more obvious conviction, that Jesus, though killed on the cross, had nonetheless ascended to heaven, not emerge as a favourable option? After all, we have already noted that Enoch and Elijah were recorded as having been transported directly to heaven. And the famous Roman senator Seneca celebrated the supposed deification, or what he called the 'pumpkinification' of the Emperor Claudius only a few years later.[3] Instead, however, the conviction that Jesus had been raised from the dead came to be affirmed as an entirely unique event, albeit foreshadowing a more general hope for the end of history. So we are brought back once again, like it or not, to the uniqueness of the event which Christians regard as the basis of their view of history and of their final destiny.

Conclusion

The problem with trying to evaluate or assess a unique claim is its uniqueness. As noted at the beginning, it is as difficult to get our heads round the claim that Jesus was raised from the dead as it is to get our heads round the beginning of the cosmos. And it is entirely challenging to accept all that the earliest Christians claim regarding what they believed happened to Jesus. The challenges include:

- An event which turned an arch persecutor of the first Christians into the most effective Christian preacher and missionary. And yet he writes so persuasively about it, and attributes his great success to the risen Jesus, who he believed had encountered and commissioned him.
- Disciples who seemed to have lost all hope yet were transformed and became effective emissaries of one decisively rejected by the leaders of his/their own people.
- A grave found empty, with no other undisturbed grave suggested as Jesus' true end, despite the hostility to the early Christian proclamation, or anything forming a decisive riposte for those unconvinced by the resurrection claims.

- A belief in resurrection – that is, not simply restoration to a life which would end in death, but resurrection to life beyond death. Why so in the case of one man when it soon became clear that it was not really the beginning of the (general) resurrection of the dead?

So, was Jesus raised from the dead? There's a lot more going for a positive answer than simple trust in the accounts of Paul and the Gospels.

Notes

Introduction

1 Genesis 5.24; 2 Kings 2.11.
2 *The Gospel of Peter* 39–40: The soldiers guarding the tomb 'saw three men come out from the sepulchre, two of them supporting the other and a cross following them, and the heads of the two reaching to heaven, but that of him who was being led reached beyond the heavens'. *The Gospel of Peter* is usually dated to the second half of the second century – J. K. Elliott, *The Apocryphal New Testament* (Oxford: Oxford University Press, 1993), 150.

1 The (only) first-hand testimony

1 The Book of Acts is usually attributed to Luke, Paul's companion for much of the story he tells in Acts. The transition from a third-person account to a first-person account ('we') every so often in the account (Acts 16.10–17; 20.5–15; 21.8–18; 27.1—28.16) is usually taken as indicating Luke's personal participation in the events described.
2 Acts 9.3–8; 22.6–11; 26.12–20.
3 It was Paul who gave the word 'gospel', meaning 'good news', and at the time usually used in the plural, its distinctive Christian sense, the gospel of Jesus' death and resurrection. Of the 76 uses of the term 'gospel' in the New Testament, 60 are in letters attributed to Paul.
4 Next to the Temple priests in Jerusalem the Pharisees were the most influential sect within first-century Judaism.
5 1 Corinthians itself is the best example.

2 The earlier claims to encounter Jesus risen from the dead

1 CE = Christian Era, is now often preferred to AD = Anno Domini ('the year of the Lord'). So also BCE = Before the Christian Era.

2 According to Luke 3.23, Jesus was 'about thirty years of age' in the fifteenth year of Emperor Tiberius Caesar (Luke 3.1), that is, about 27 or 28 CE. Jesus' two- or three-year ministry then means that the 14th Nisan 30 was the most likely date of his crucifixion.

3 Galatians 1.18; Acts 9.26–28.

4 E.g. *The Apocryphon of James* (550 days), and *Ascension of Isaiah* 9.16 (545 days), which could allow the inclusion of the appearance to Paul.

5 To maintain belief in the virginity of Mary, Jesus' mother, the tradition developed that James was Jesus' half-brother.

6 Acts 12.17; 15.13; 21.18; Galatians 1.19; 2.9, 12.

7 It is striking that 'the twelve' is so firmly fixed in the tradition, despite Judas's betrayal and suicide. Acts resolves the possible inconsistency by narrating the election of a successor to Judas (Acts 1.15–26); but that was after Luke's account of the completion of the resurrection appearances (1.9–11).

8 Matthew 28.16–20; Luke 24.36–49; John 20.19–23, 26–29; 21.1–23; Acts 1.3–11.

3 What are we to make of the tensions between the several accounts?

1 The Jewish historian Josephus indicates what was probably the typical prejudice of the time: 'From women let no evidence be accepted, because of the levity and temerity of their sex' (*Antiquities* 4.219). Luke evidently shared the same scepticism (Luke 24.11). See further my *Jesus Remembered* (Eerdmans, 2003), §18.2a.

2 See my *Beginning from Jerusalem* (Eerdmans, 2009), §29.6.

3 The point is slightly odd, since John does not in fact include an account of the last supper, though the discourse in John 6 may well be intended to serve the same purpose.

4 2 Corinthians 1.19; 1 Thessalonians 1.1; 2 Thessalonians 1.1; also 1 Peter 5.12.
5 Notably 2 Corinthians 8.23 and Philippians 2.25.
6 1 Corinthians 1.12; 3.4–6, 22.
7 Intriguingly, Luke had no qualms in using the same word to describe visions as such – as in Acts 9.10, 12; 10.3, 17, 19; 11.5; 16.9–10; 18.9.
8 Matthew 28.9; Luke 24.31, 36, 51; John 20.19, 26; Acts 1.9.

4 The empty tomb tradition

1 Matthew 27.57–58; Mark 15.43; Luke 23.50–52; John 19.38.
2 Matthew 27.59–60; Mark 15.45–46; Luke 23.53–54; John 19.39–41.
3 Matthew and Mark agree that the women were Mary Magdalene and 'the other Mary' (Matthew 27.61)/'Mary the mother of Joses' (Mark 15.47). John does not mention any women at this point but has the Nicodemus of John 3 acting in an equivalent role (John 19.39–40).
4 Mark 16.4; Luke 24.2; John 20.1.
5 Matthew 27.56, 61; 28.1; Mark 15.40, 47; 16.1; Luke 24.10; John 19.25; 20.1, 11–18.
6 Matthew 27.56; Mark 15.40; 16.1; Luke 24.10.
7 Most notably 1 Corinthians 15.4; but see also e.g. Acts 10.40; Romans 10.9; Galatians 1.1; Ephesians 1.20; 1 Thessalonians 1.10; 1 Peter 1.21.
8 Matthew 27.33; Mark 15.22; John 19.17.
9 Mark 15.15–19.

5 Why 'resurrection'?

1 In the Mishnah, resurrection has become an article of faith for the rabbis, the successors of the Pharisees (*m. Sanhedrin* 10.1).
2 Mark 8.31; 9.31; 10.33–34.
3 Cassius Dio, *Roman History* 61.35.

Further reading

Allison, D. C. *Resurrecting Jesus: The Earliest Christian Tradition and its Interpreters*. London: T & T Clark, 2005.

Bayer, H. F. *Jesus' Predictions of Vindication and Resurrection*. WUNT 2.20; Tübingen: Mohr Siebeck, 1986.

Brown, R. E. *The Virginal Conception and Bodily Resurrection of Jesus*. New York: Paulist Press, 1973.

Bryan, C. *The Resurrection of the Messiah*. Oxford: Oxford University Press, 2011.

von Campenhausen, H. 'The Events of Easter and the Empty Tomb', in *Tradition and Life in the Church*. London: Collins, 1968, pp. 42–89.

Craig, W. L. *Assessing the New Testament Evidence for the Historicity of the Resurrection of Jesus*. Lampeter: Edwin Mellen, 1989.

Dunn, J. D. G. *Jesus Remembered*. Grand Rapids, MI: Eerdmans, 2003. Part Five.

Longenecker, R. N. (ed.) *Life in the Face of Death: The Resurrection Message of the New Testament*. Grand Rapids, MI: Eerdmans, 1998.

Lüdemann, G. *The Resurrection of Jesus*. London: SCM Press, 1994.

Perkins, P. *Resurrection: New Testament Witness and Contemporary Reflection*. London: Chapman, 1984.

Price, R. M. and Lowder, J. J. (eds) *The Empty Tomb: Jesus Beyond the Grave*. Amherst, NY: Prometheus Books, 2005.

Vermes, G. *The Resurrection: History and Myth*. New York: Doubleday, 2008.

Wright, N. T. *The Resurrection of the Son of God*. London: SPCK, 2003.